Dive, Dolphin!

Shira Evans

NATIONAL GEOGRAPHIC

Washington, D.C.

Vocabulary Tree

DOLPHINS

WHERE THEY LIVE	WHAT THEY DO	WHAT THEY HAVE
ocean	dive	flipper
river	swim	fin
	hunt	tail
	play	
	leap	
	jump	
	breathe	

Dive, dolphin!

3

There are many kinds of dolphins.
Some have long beaks.

Some have short beaks.

These dolphins have stripes.

This dolphin has spots.

Some dolphins live in oceans.

Others live in rivers.

tail

fin

flipper

All dolphins have
flippers, a fin, and a tail.

Dolphins swim together.

They work as a
team to hunt fish.

Dolphins like to play with things they find in the water.

This dolphin plays
with seaweed.

They also like to
leap and jump.

A dolphin gets air through its blowhole. Then it dives back down into the water.

Dolphins need to breathe.

They come to the top of
the water to get air.

Dive, dolphin!

Dolphin Habitat Map

Dolphins live in oceans and rivers around the world. Here's where these dolphins live.

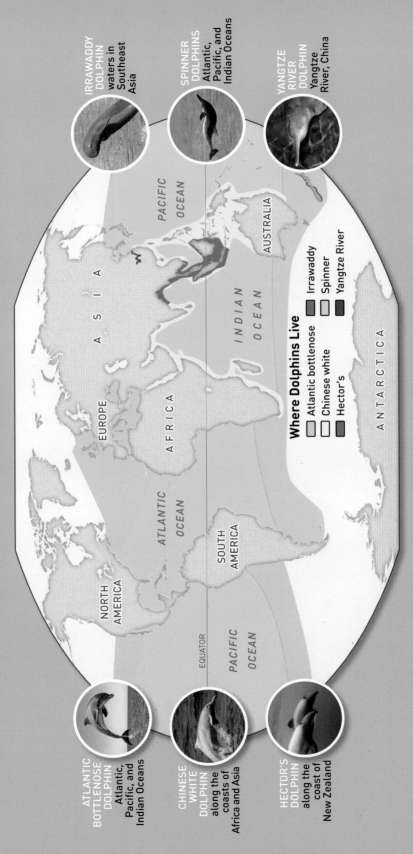

IRRAWADDY DOLPHIN waters in Southeast Asia

SPINNER DOLPHINS Atlantic, Pacific, and Indian Oceans

YANGTZE RIVER DOLPHIN Yangtze River, China

ATLANTIC BOTTLENOSE DOLPHIN Atlantic, Pacific, and Indian Oceans

CHINESE WHITE DOLPHIN along the coasts of Africa and Asia

HECTOR'S DOLPHIN along the coast of New Zealand

PACIFIC OCEAN

ASIA

AUSTRALIA

EUROPE

AFRICA

INDIAN OCEAN

ATLANTIC OCEAN

NORTH AMERICA

SOUTH AMERICA

ANTARCTICA

PACIFIC OCEAN

EQUATOR

Where Dolphins Live

- Atlantic bottlenose
- Chinese white
- Hector's
- Irrawaddy
- Spinner
- Yangtze River

YOUR TURN!

Match the word to the photo. Use your finger to make a line from the word to the photo.

PLAY

JUMP

HUNT

BREATHE

The answer is on the next page.

Published by National Geographic Partners, LLC, Washington, D.C. 20036. All rights reserved. Reproduction in whole or in part without written permission of the publisher is prohibited.

Designed by Rachel Kenny

Library of Congress Cataloging-in-Publication Data

Names: Evans, Shira, author. | National Geographic Society (U.S.)
Title: Dive, dolphin! / by Shira Evans.
Description: 1st edition. | Washington, DC : National Geographic Partners,
  2016. | Series: National geographic readers | Audience: Ages 2-5.
Identifiers: LCCN 2016005543| ISBN 9781426324406 (pbk. : alk. paper) | ISBN
  9781426324413 (library binding : alk. paper)
Subjects: LCSH: Dolphins--Juvenile literature.
Classification: LCC QL737.C432 E93 2016 | DDC 599.53--dc23
LC record available at https://lccn.loc.gov/2016005543

Photo Credits
Cover, Brandon Cole; 1, Willyam Bradberry/Shutterstock; 2-3, Hiroya Minakuchi/Minden Pictures; 4, Mark Carwardine/Minden Pictures; 5, Greg Boreham (TrekLightly)/Getty Images; 6, Brandon Cole/Kimball Stock; 7, Jim Abernethy/Getty Images; 8, Doug Perrine/SeaPics.com; 9, Kevin Schafer/Minden Pictures; 10-11, Jeff Rotman/Getty Images; 12-13, Alexander Safonov/Getty Images; 14-15, Reinhard Dirscherl/Minden Pictures; 16-17, Stuart Westmorland/Getty Images; 18-19, Flip Nicklin/Minden Pictures; 20-21, Juergen and Christine Sohns/Getty Images; 22 (UP LE), Roland Seitre/Nature Picture Library; 22 (UP CTR), Flip Nicklin/Minden Pictures; 22 (UP RT), Roland Seitre/Minden Pictures; 22 (LO LE), Mike Hill/Getty Images; 22 (LO CTR), Thomas Jefferson/SeaPics.com; 22 (LO RT), Tobias Bernhard Raff/Minden Pictures; 23 (UP), Stuart Westmorland/Getty Images; 23 (UP CTR), Flip Nicklin/Minden Pictures; 23 (LO CTR), Reinhard Dirscherl/Minden Pictures; 23 (LO), Alexander Safonov/Getty Images; 24 (UP), Jeff Rotman/Getty Images; 24 (inset, UP), Stuart Westmorland/Getty Images; 24 (inset, UP CTR), Flip Nicklin/Minden Pictures; 24 (inset, LO CTR), Reinhard Dirscherl/Minden Pictures; 24 (inset, LO), Alexander Safonov/Getty Images

Printed in the United States of America
16/WOR/1

ANSWER:

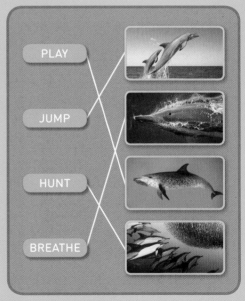

PLAY

JUMP

HUNT

BREATHE

National Geographic supports K–12 educators with ELA Common Core Resources. Visit natgeoed.org /commoncore for more information.